I0189992

Prayers For Healing

A Service, Prayers, And Bible Readings

Eva Juliuson

CSS Publishing Company, Inc., Lima, Ohio

PRAYERS FOR HEALING

Copyright © 2001 by
CSS Publishing Company, Inc.
Lima, Ohio

The original purchaser may photocopy material in this publication for use as it was in-
tended (i.e., worship material for worship use; educational material for classroom use;
dramatic material for staging or production). No additional permission is required from
the publisher for such copying by the original purchaser only. Inquiries should be ad-
dressed to: Permissions, CSS Publishing Company, Inc., P.O. Box 4503, Lima, Ohio 45802-
4503.

Scripture quotations are taken from the *Holy Bible*, New Living Translation, copyright ©
1996. Used by permission of Tyndale House Publishers, Inc., Wheaton, Illinois 60189.
All rights reserved.

For more information about CSS Publishing Company resources, visit our website at
www.csspub.com.

ISBN 0-7880-1799-3   PRINTED IN U.S.A.

Is anyone among you suffering? He should keep on praying about it ... Is anyone sick? He should call for the elders of the church and they should pray over him and pour a little oil upon him, calling on the Lord to heal him. And the prayer, if offered in faith, will heal him, for the Lord will make him well.

James 5:14-16

Table Of Contents

Why Pray For Healing?

Remember the lame man who was carried on a stretcher to Jesus? His friends cared so deeply about the man that they went to great lengths to bring him before the Lord for healing. The crowd was too thick for them to get through to Jesus, so they cut a hole in the roof so they could lower their friend down to where Jesus was. Jesus was touched by their love for their friend and by their faith. He healed the man.

There is pain, suffering, and illness all around us today. We all have loved ones who are suffering with some disease or condition. They need us to pray for them. They need us to bring them before the Lord, for they are often too weak to get there themselves. It takes all their energy just to deal with their illness. It's up to us, as their friends, family, and church, to pick them up and bring them before the Lord for healing. We can carry them to the Lord in prayer.

You may feel helpless and your prayers may seem weak, but praying is the most powerful thing you can do for them. As someone who for four years stood beside a husband who was dying, I cannot stress how very important other people's prayers are to those who are suffering.

We have been asked by the Lord to pray for those who are sick and to bear one another's burdens. The most powerful thing we can do is pray for those persons. Not only do we need to pray in private for them, but we need to gather around them, lay hands upon them, and lift them up to our Lord. They need our strength and our prayers. You may not feel very strong. That's okay! You only need to be strong enough to carry them to the Lord and place them in his hands. God will do the rest.

What You Need
For Healing Prayers

Prayerful attitudes: Each person involved should come humbly before the Lord, yet boldly trusting that God's will be done.

Towel: Wrap a towel around the sick person's shoulders so the oil doesn't stain clothes.

Olive oil: Oil is to be poured over the person's head or dabbed on in some fashion. The anointing of oil symbolizes the anointing of the Holy Spirit.

Tissues: There may be tears.

How Do We Pray For Healing?

The Bible gives us certain guidelines to follow in praying for healing. In James 5:13-16, it tells us to call on the elders in the church to pray for the person and to pour oil over him/her. This can be done in a formal church service, a home, a hospital bed, or a nursing home. The place does not matter, but the attitude does.

This prayer service can be done with two or more present. It may be quiet and small, yet powerful; or it may be done with a whole congregation with one or more persons being prayed for. Personalized, specific prayer should be offered for each person.

Ask all participants (the one being prayed for and those who are praying) to open their hearts to the Holy Spirit. Ask that everyone agree in prayer. As each person prays, the others present should be agreeing together for that same prayer.

This service offers a guideline of scriptures to pray. God's word is used as a pattern of prayer because his word will not go out without results. It is already lined up with the will of God. When we pray using scripture, we are agreeing with God's promises and asking for those things for the person for whom we are praying.

There may be those present who do not know how to pray or who feel uncomfortable praying out loud. This form will help those persons become a part in praying for healing. You may read the scripture just as it is written or you may personalize it for the person you are praying for by inserting his/her name. If the Spirit moves you to add to the printed prayer, follow the Holy Spirit's promptings, for he knows how to pray when we don't.

Each person should lay his/her hand upon the sick person. Have copies of the prayer service available so each participant can pray as his/her turn comes. Follow the circle around the person to pray in turn.

Note About Prayers For Healing

Great care should be taken not to limit God in the way he heals. God may truly heal instantaneously, or God may heal the spirit, giving the person the peace and grace he/she needs to handle the pain and suffering. We cannot tell God what is best for anyone's life. Only God knows his plans and the good it will bring about. Our Heavenly Father uses many strange and wonderful ways to heal. There is no doubt that this prayer service will bring about healing. It's up to us to open our eyes to see the healing God brings about and what form it will take. God may immediately heal the body, or he may give the tired and weary soul energy and renewal so the person can continue to endure until God's glorious plan is revealed through this illness.

The most important attitude we can have as we pray for healing is to submit ourselves to God. We need to pray until we are willing (and even desire) that *God's* will be done. There is a temptation for us to tell God how we want our prayers answered. We need to strive to bring the hurting person to the Lord and let God do what is absolutely best in that person's life.

May the Lord bless you for putting your compassion to work in the form of prayers. Thank you for being the kind of friend who will lift up this one who is weak and hurting and carry him/her to the Lord so God can touch the one in need with his healing hands.

Prayers For Healing Service

Praise God!

Father, we come before you praising your holy name and acknowledging that you are the only one who can truly heal _____ (name of person for whom you are praying).

"Praise the Lord, my soul, and never forget all the good he has done: he is the one who forgives all your sins, the one who heals all your diseases." *Psalm 103:2-3*

"Praise the God and Father of our Lord Jesus Christ! He is the Father who is compassionate and the Father who gives comfort. He comforts us when we suffer. That is why whenever other people suffer, we are able to comfort them by using the same comfort we have received from God." *2 Corinthians 1:3-4*

"God is our refuge and strength, an ever-present help in times of trouble. That is why we are not afraid even when the earth quakes or the mountains topple into the depths of the sea." *Psalm 46:1-2*

"Praise the Lord, my soul! All my being, praise his holy name. Praise the Lord, my soul, and do not forget how kind he is. He forgives all my sins and heals all my diseases. He keeps me from the grave and blesses me with love and mercy." *Psalm 103:1-4*

"Everything that happens in this world happens at the time God chooses: he sets ... the time for killing and the time for healing." *Ecclesiastes 3:1, 3*

"I cried to you for help, O Lord my God, and you healed me; you kept me from the grave. I was on my way to the depths before, but you restored my life." *Psalm 30:2, 3*

Confession

Father, let us quietly confess anything you bring to our mind which stands between you and us, so we might receive your forgiveness and stand holy and pure before you as we ask for healing for _____.

(A few moments of silence for silent confession.)

"Come, let's talk this over! says the Lord; no matter how deep the stain of your sins, I can take it out and make you as clean as freshly fallen snow. Even if you are stained as red as crimson, I can make you as white as wool!"   *Isaiah 1:18*

"If we say we have no sin, we are only fooling ourselves, and refusing to accept the truth. But, if we confess our sins to him, he can be depended upon to forgive us and to cleanse us from every wrong."
1 John 1:8, 9

"But, dearly beloved friends, if our consciences are clear, we can come to the Lord with perfect assurance and trust, and get whatever we ask for because we are obeying him and doing the things that please him."   *1 John 3:21, 22*

"Return, all of you, who have turned away from the Lord; he will heal you and make you faithful."   *Isaiah 53:5*

Thanksgiving

Father, we give our deep thanks to you for the right and the opportunity to bring _____ before you so we can ask for your healing touch on him/her. We even thank you for the hidden blessings which have come with this condition, for we know there are deep treasures found in the dark valley when it's walked with you, Lord. Thank you for the way you have been with _____ all through this time. We thank you for just loving _____ and never leaving him/her. We thank you for the strength we've seen in _____ as he/she has gone through this.

Thank you, Father, for the forgiveness of our sins, and for the honor and privilege to pray for _____ and his/her family, for we know his/her family is greatly burdened also. Thank you for the unity we share as we join together to pray for comfort, peace, and good health for _____.

"Never worry about anything. But in every situation let God know what you need in prayers and requests while giving thanks."
Philippians 4:6

"Whatever happens, give thanks, because it is God's will in Jesus Christ that you do this."
1 Thessalonians 5:18

"God has given you the privilege not only to believe in Christ, but also to suffer for him."
Philippians 1:29

"We know that all things work together for the good of those who love God — those whom he has called according to his plan."
Romans 8:28

"The Lord will support _____ on his/her sickbed. You will restore this person to health when he/she is ill."
Psalm 41:3

"The one who loves us gives us an overwhelming victory in all these difficulties."
Romans 8:37

Intercession

(Anoint with oil at this time.)

Father, we anoint _____ with this oil. Let your Holy Spirit pour over him/her and bathe him/her with your healing touch. We pray for him/her to be strengthened, healed, and given all he/she needs in you. Lord, you know we don't exactly know what to pray for, but we trust that your Holy Spirit is here to intercede for us and for _____. We totally place _____ in your hands, knowing that you know exactly what he/she needs and what is best for his/her life. Let your will be done.

"At the same time, the Spirit also helps us in our weakness, because we don't know how to pray for what we need. But the Spirit intercedes along with our groans that cannot be expressed in words."   *Romans 8:26*

"Even though _____ walks through the dark valley of the shadow of death, because you are with him/her, he/she will fear no harm. Your rod and your staff give him/her courage."
Psalm 23:4

"Relieve _____'s troubled heart, and bring him/her out of his/her distress."   *Psalm 25:17*

"When _____ walks through fire, he/she will not be burned, and the flames will not harm him/her."   *Isaiah 43:2*

We pray for _____ to have a joyful heart: "A joyful heart is good medicine, but depression drains one's strength."
Proverbs 17:22

We pray for strength for _____ and his/her family: "Be strong, all who wait with hope for the Lord, and let your heart be courageous."   *Psalm 31:24*

"I am convinced that God, who began this good work in you, will carry it through to completion on the day of Christ Jesus."
Philippians 1:6

We pray for patience as _____ and his/her family wait for the Lord to work all things together for good: "They will walk and not grow tired. Don't be afraid because I am with you. Don't be intimidated, I am your God. I will strengthen you. I will help you. I will support you with my victorious right hand."

Isaiah 41:10

"_____ can do everything through Christ who strengthens him/her."

Philippians 4:13

"When I called, you answered me. You made me bold by strengthening my soul."

Psalm 138:3

"But he told me, 'My kindness is all you need. My power is strongest when you are weak.' So I will brag even more about my weakness in order that Christ's power will live in me. Therefore, I accept my weakness, mistreatment, hardship, persecution, and difficulties suffered for Christ. It's clear that when I'm weak, I'm strong."

2 Corinthians 12:9-10

"_____'s suffering is light and temporary and is producing him/her an eternal glory that is greater than anything we can imagine."

2 Corinthians 4:17

"Before they call, I will answer. While they are still speaking I will hear."

Isaiah 65:24

"I know the plans that I have for _____, declares the Lord. They are plans for peace and not disaster, plans to give him/her a future filled with hope."

Jeremiah 29:11

"We are healed by the punishment he suffered, made whole by the blows he received."

Isaiah 53:5

"Lord, heal me and I will be completely well; rescue me and I will be perfectly safe. You are the one I praise!"

Jeremiah 17:14

"He himself took our sickness and carried our diseases."

Matthew 8:17

"The Lord will help them when they are sick and restore them to health." *Psalm 41:3*

"My child, pay attention to what I say. Listen to my words. Never let them get away from you. Remember them and keep them in your heart. They will give life and health to anyone who understands them." *Proverbs 4:20-22*

"I will make you well again. I will heal your wounds." *Jeremiah 30:17*

"But for you who obey me, my saving power will rise on you like the sun and bring healing like the sun's rays." *Malachi 4:2*

"I, the Lord, the God of your ancestor David, have heard your prayer and seen your tears. I will heal you...." *2 Kings 20:5*

"Come to me, all who are tired from carrying heavy loads and I will give you rest." *Matthew 11:28*

"He is the healer of the brokenhearted. He is the one who bandages their wounds." *Psalm 147:13*

Father, we praise you and thank you for allowing us to bring _____ before you so you can touch him/her and make him/her whole once more. We know you will do this. We do not know what form this healing will take. Only you are God. Only you know what is best in _____'s life. Lord, we put ourselves and _____ in your hands. If it is your will that he/she carries this illness, then, Lord, we know you will give him/her all he/she needs to go through it. We know you will be with him/her.
We know your ways are not our ways, Lord, and we trust that you will do what is absolutely best. However you answer these prayers for healing, we love you and honor you for you alone are our Lord God Almighty! Thank you for aligning our will to yours. Let your will be done, Lord! Amen.

16

www.ingramcontent.com/pod-product-compliance
Lightning Source LLC
Chambersburg PA
CBHW071814020426
42331CB00009B/2498

* 9 780788 017995 *